¢ENTSIBLE MEALS
How to feed your family for LESS

¢ENTSIBLE MEALS
How to feed your family for **LESS**

Lorae Bowden

CFI
Springville, Utah

ISBN 13: 978-1-59955-305-4

Published by CFI, an imprint of Cedar Fort, Inc., 2373 W. 700 S., Springville, UT 84663
Distributed by Cedar Fort, Inc. www.cedarfort.com

LIBRARY OF CONGRESS CATALOGING-IN-PUBLICATION DATA

Bowden, Lorae.
   Centsible meals : how to feed your family for less / Lorae Bowden.
      p. cm.
   ISBN 978-1-59955-305-4 (acid-free paper)
   1. Low budget cookery. I. Title.

   TX652.B673 2009
   641.5'52--dc22

                         2009017288

Cover design by Megan Whittier
Cover design © 2009 by Lyle Mortimer
Edited and typeset by Megan E. Welton

Printed in the United States of America

10 9 8 7 6 5 4 3 2 1

Printed on acid-free paper

Dedication

To my parents, Tom and Louann Hunsaker,
who taught me common sense in the first place.

And to my husband, Jared,
for his added knowledge, skills, and enduring encouragement.

Contents

Contents

1. Eating ¢entsibly

We are indeed much more than what we eat, but what we eat can nevertheless help us to be much more than what we are.

—Adelle Davis

I once watched a television show that discussed poverty-stricken American families. This documentary made the point that the United States welfare system was not giving destitute families enough money to buy food. I specifically recall one family being interviewed. There were six people in the household, and they were receiving seven hundred dollars in food stamps monthly. They were going without meals because they ran out of food stamps before the end of every month.

I reflected that I feed my family of eight on two hundred dollars a month—less than a dollar per person per day—with no welfare involved. Seven hundred dollars seemed like a luxury to me. Obviously the people on television were not properly planning for and spending their stamps wisely.

In the years following that particular television show, I have observed similar examples of financial and nutritional distress in families because of faulty money management. It seems that much of America's poverty is not a lack of money, but a lack of basic knowledge about the planning and preparation of filling, healthful, and inexpensive meals. Many families simply do not know how to eat for less.

Humans must eat to survive, but how and what we eat is conditioned by our upbringing as well as social norms and expectations. By the time we are adults, we have been taught to like and eat certain foods. Most of us have learned to crave and expect specific foods at regular intervals throughout the day. It naturally follows that we buy food according to our eating habits.

In the United States, we are also confronted with advertising. Restaurants and fast food chains send weekly flyers, and we regularly see tempting food on television commercials. Statistics show that Americans eat out an average of five times per week. Because this is only an average, it means that for all of us who don't eat out, there are many who eat out much more often than five times per week. Almost 50 percent of every dollar spent on food is spent at a restaurant.[1]

Companies actively promote recipes that use their products. They advertise recipe contests and give away free recipe cards that are often in grocery store aisles next to their commodity. Almost every boxed or bagged item at the grocery store has a recipe on the packaging. On cold cereal boxes, I often find muffin or bread recipes that use that particular cereal.

Many recipes and recipe books not only suggest which specific brand of food to use, but involve ingredients that are often pre-made mixes, or foods made exclusively by a particular company. For example, you probably have a cake recipe that starts with a cake mix but has you add a few other ingredients in addition to water, oil, and eggs, to enhance the original cake. I have a citrus bundt cake recipe that starts with a lemon cake mix. Do you have a chicken recipe that involves stuffing mix? Or a soup recipe that includes a frozen bagged vegetable medley?

Forty years ago these recipes would have seemed ludicrous. Today they are standard practice. Much of our culture seems to have forgotten that it is possible—and simple—to make cakes from scratch. Most people don't realize that it is much less expensive to keep a variety of fresh vegetables on hand than it is to buy bags of frozen specialty ensembles.

Some families make headline news because they save hundreds of dollars by using coupons to buy brand-name products. Did you know that many store-brand products are made in the same factories as the brand-name products and cost less even after a coupon reduction?

Thanks, in part, to consumer advertising, we have lots of good variety in our modern diet. We have come a long way from the potatoes-and-boiled-cabbage meals of our ancestors. However, maybe the average household cook has lost valuable arts in the process—creativity, simplicity, and the knowledge of how to get a lot for a little.

It seems like most people in today's world are trying to make their money stretch. Many are dealing with financial hardships—credit card debt, high mortgage payments, and so forth. We can turn on the TV, walk into a bookstore, or get on the Internet to find a wealth of advice about lowering debt or consolidating loans or getting better gas mileage. But there seems to be little advice about eating more simply or combining resources to get more mileage out of our food dollar. Many people clip coupons, buy into diet plans, live on processed foods, and go on welfare programs to conserve money. There is nothing horribly wrong with any of these, but I believe there is a better, healthier alternative that can save families more money and make them happier and more self-sufficient. The solution is learning how to plan, budget, and use basic inexpensive ingredients in cooking. And it's easier and much more fun than you might think.

I grew up in the recession of the early eighties. My mother, a conscientious and dedicated homemaker, learned how to use whole wheat, beans, and potatoes. She understood the difference between needs and wants, and inexpensive versus cheap. While we children may sometimes have wished for the chips and white bread of our friends' lunches at school, we never went hungry. She raised eleven healthy, happy children. None of us are overweight nor do we have diet-related health problems. Best of all, our mother passed down the skills, knowledge, and appreciation of healthful and thrifty food preparation to all of us. Because of these skills, I can afford to be a stay-at-home mom while my husband goes to graduate school and we live on his stipend—intended for young single grad students—with our family of eight.

The purpose of this book is to present principles and practices to help you save money on the food you eat. I firmly believe that most families can eat well on a budget of a dollar per person per day. Calculate how much you spend monthly on food and eating out. Subtract a dollar a day for each family member. What would you like to do with the resulting extra money? Write it down and post it on your fridge as an incentive. Now read this book and consider each suggestion.

In this book, you will find principles for proper planning and savvy shopping. You will know how to create well-rounded and filling meals and how to craft your own recipes. You will learn about basic food preparation, as well as tips for cutting costs on many non-food household items.

Perhaps some of these recommendations you are already doing, or at least will be easy to incorporate into your lifestyle. Some will take contemplation and evaluation, and there may be some trial and error before they become a part of your everyday routine. You might feel there are some not worth trying, but I encourage you to give them a chance. You may find you like the change.

These suggestions have played a big part in the making of my own family's lifestyle. We have fun together trying (and sometimes failing at) new things. We spend quality time working together. I am consciously sharing not only cooking and budgeting skills with my own children, but also good values like work and responsibility, as well as appreciation for the world around them and the courage to try new things; these are all nice side effects of frugality and creativity in the kitchen.

More spending money, better health, happier children, and a simple, more wholesome all-around lifestyle—here are just some of the advantages of following the suggestions in this book. You can enjoy spending your hard-earned money on real memories that won't disappear by next week, and you will feel the immense satisfaction that comes from knowing you have the skills necessary to be self-reliant in order to get the most out of your dollar.

2. Less Processed = Less Money

*Three Rules of Work: Out of clutter find simplicity;
from discord find harmony; in the middle of difficulty lies
opportunity.*

—**Albert Einstein**

We live in a society of thirty-minute meals and quick fixes. Many people don't realize that real cooking is not generally hard or time-consuming—even if using the most basic ingredients. In fact, at least one study showed that there was very little preparation time difference between families who prepared dinner from scratch and those that used pre-packaged items.[2] Stock your pantry with dried peas and beans, regular white and brown rice, regular oatmeal, sacks of potatoes and onions, cornmeal, flour, salt, and some spices, and you have an endless variety of possible meals.

The bottom line here is to evaluate what you buy and see if you can make it from scratch for less.

Get Rid of Boxes and Bags

Before you buy a box or bag mix, consider what is in it. Can you make it on your own, or at least get pretty close? Chances are, you can make that meal for less money and fast enough to get dinner ready on time.

For example, making your own rice or noodle skillet takes exactly the same amount of time as the box variety. You just have to know what flavorings go in it.

Have you thought about the "Meat" Helper boxed dinners? The company actually makes you supply the most expensive ingredient (hamburger) and provides only noodles and flavoring. If you did it yourself, it would take no more time than the mix, and you could adjust the servings to fit your family size. See the recipe section of this book for some good noodle and rice box dinner substitutes.

Okay, so cutting vegetables for that stir-fry will take five or six minutes longer than just opening a bag of frozen vegetables. If you don't have time, cut them up some Saturday afternoon, or some evening while you're watching TV, and have them in the fridge ready to go into a stir-fry. Fresh vegetables don't take any longer to cook than the frozen ones.

Instead of buying a box of potato flakes, pick up a bag of potatoes—a lot more potato for the same price.

A package of salad will feed my family for two meals, but a head of lettuce is half the price and will feed us for three or four meals.

Dried beans are much more cost effective than canned. Soaking them may require thinking ahead, but it doesn't take much more actual preparation time than draining a can does.

Flour is a lot cheaper than Bisquick. Is it really that hard to add baking powder yourself?

Many people would not attempt to make a cake without a mix, but did you know that you are still adding about half of the total ingredients when you add water, oil, and eggs? Plus, you probably have all the necessary components sitting in your cupboard already.

Soups

Prepared soups are generally expensive and unnecessary. Try duplicating your favorite soup with ingredients you have on hand. Better yet, make up your own yummy concoction. Soups were originally a catch-all food—to be made out of leftovers or things people had on hand.

Soups are usually made from a basic base. For a good broth soup, start with beef or chicken broth, which can be made out of bouillon cubes or base.

Add whatever you have that sounds good. I usually make my soups hearty with rice, noodles, potatoes, or beans, and then add whatever vegetables I have. Pearled barley, alphabet noodles, and even whole wheat noodles can add variety and interest to a soup.

We like thick soups, even if they are mostly made of broth, so I mix a couple of tablespoons of cornstarch in enough cold water to make it pourable, and whisk it into the bubbling soup just before I serve it.

If you like cream soups, start with a simple roux or white sauce recipe. Chicken bouillon cubes add good flavor to most cream soups, even if there is no chicken involved. To cut back on cost of milk and cream, I use part water and part milk.

You can throw everything into a crock-pot in the morning, or start a half hour before dinner.

Soups are fun to play with. There are endless varieties of vegetables and seasonings. They are also adaptable to time constraints.

Less Processed = Healthier, Too!

By making your own meals from scratch, you avoid artificial ingredients like flavorings, colorings, and preservatives. Many of these are believed to be potentially toxic and even cancer-causing as they build up in our bodies. By preparing your own dishes, you can also avoid the high amounts of sodium often found in mixes and packaged or canned food.

Eat the skins with your potatoes. Make roasted potato wedges instead of French fries (see recipe on page 67). Leave the skins on for soups. Did you know that potatoes mash just as well when you dice and boil them with the skins on? Potato skins have loads of vitamins, minerals, and fiber not found in the white flesh. Besides, it saves time if you don't have to peel them for everything.

Brown rice is one of the most nutrient-rich grains in the world today. White rice, on the other hand, has had a lot of the good stuff taken out. It's similar to the difference between whole-wheat flour and white flour. I didn't eat much brown rice growing up, but on one of my "let's eat healthy" kicks after my husband and I got married, I decided some brown rice in our diet would be a good change. My husband wasn't raised on it either and claimed he did not care for it in the least. I knew this might be a tricky change for both of us. I started by adding brown rice to soups where it would be less easily noticed. Then I tried using part brown, part white rice in flavored pilafs. (Note: brown rice takes longer to cook, so if you use part brown, part white, cook the brown first and add the white the last twenty minutes.) There were no complaints, so I started making all brown rice pilafs and going half and half on plain rice for stir fry and gravy. Now we use brown rice almost exclusively. The whole family now enjoys brown rice equally as well as white.

Try whole grain pastas and breads. We were lucky enough to receive both a bread mixer and pasta maker for our wedding. They have held up nobly through thirteen years of use and made it possible for us to eat well with little money.

Healthier is less expensive! If you think some of these healthy tips mean more money, consider a few things. More fiber in your diet means it takes less food to fill you up. It also means a more regular digestive system and less chance of developing colon cancer or needing laxative drugs.

Healthy diets mean less sickness and fewer medical bills. Consider any vitamin supplements you may be taking. While I believe supplements are healthier than nothing, the real food source is always a better choice than a manufactured replica. I was once concerned about my calcium intake and thought about buying calcium supplement pills to make up for the deficiency. I priced the pills and realized I could buy enough milk and cheese (things I considered pricey) to get my recommended daily amount for less than the calcium tablets would cost.

Motivation

My kids love to play "Pioneer." They borrow bread, drink water from an old tin cup, and pretend to kill bears and deer for survival. I will admit that it helps me to think about early American settlers when I shop and cook. There is something inspiring about people who made do with what they had. Thinking about them makes me want to be like them. Whatever helps you feel like a "granola" or a pioneer may help boost your desire to live frugally. Read *Little House on the Prairie*, or check out some ancient country cookbooks from your library. Spend a quiet, uninterrupted five minutes a day thinking about how good these changes will be for your wallet, skin, and waistline. Don't forget to keep the calculated amount of food money you will save posted on your fridge. Make sure you already have plans for that extra money—a vacation, a new couch, whatever. Do what it takes to stay inspired and committed to get back to basic foods and save money.

3. Basiç Fillers

As you simplify your life, the laws of the universe will be simpler; solitude will not be solitude, poverty will not be poverty, nor weakness weakness.

—Henry David Thoreau

A good meal is built around basic fillers. A filler is what guarantees that no one will walk away hungry from a meal. It should be versatile, inexpensive, store well, and offer good nutrition. There are four good fillers—grains, beans, rice, and potatoes. Yes, they are all carbohydrates, but they can all be good carbs.

A quick blurb about carbs here: Carbohydrates have taken a bad rap in the media and diet world. Carbohydrates give your body energy. The reason they often get a bad name is that many people eat white flours and pasta, white rice, and potatoes soaked in grease and fat. These are generally empty carbs that have few nutrients and convert quickly into sugars in your body. If not used immediately as energy, they can turn into stored fat. Americans are not obese because of bread and pasta. Many people throughout the world eat rice, beans, and bread as staple foods and are not obese. The difference for Americans, besides simply eating too much, is that we often don't get our carbs from whole grain. Whole grains and vegetables not only supply energy, but they have fiber and loads of vitamins and minerals as well. Whole grains help keep your metabolism high, your blood sugar even, and your energy level constant. A good diet will use these as a foundation for eating well.

Other good news is that beans, brown rice, whole grains, and potatoes are all relatively inexpensive and satisfying. Your family can eat a lot, and it won't cost you very much per serving. Try to use a filler food as the main dish of your meal and augment it with other foods.

- An example of a hearty meal using a filler food would be stir-fry. Lots of rice to satiate, topped with vegetables, and a little meat, if you choose. Serve some fruit slices on the side, and you have a great meal.
- A big pot of baked beans makes a great filler accompanied by a veggie and fruit and a slice of bread.
- Bread itself can be a filler for a meal. My family loves homemade whole wheat bread, hot out of the oven. If I make enough, we can eat bread topped with butter and honey, a side dish of veggies and apple slices, and call it a meal.

Organize!

I am an organizer, and everyone likes variety, so I try not to use the same filler two nights in a row. I have found it easy to assign each staple to a night of the week. Mondays are rice night, Tuesdays are beans, and so on. Weekends are less structured, so we eat leftovers or fix something to suit whatever our mood may be that day. Because I design meals around certain fillers, I file my recipes accordingly. You will find that the recipes in the back of this book are arranged in sections for rice, beans, pasta, potatoes, and whole grains.

I find that menu planning is easier when I can look at my recipes and assign different rice dishes to all the Mondays in the month. You may not want to be quite so structured. Feel free to work with your personality as far as organization. The principle here is that a meal should let the more expensive parts compliment the main, inexpensive part. That is sound financial advice as well as sound nutritional advice.

4. Homemade Breads

*Talk of joy: there may be things better than beef stew
and baked potatoes and home-made bread—there may be.*

—David Gayson

Bread is the staff of life. Even in today's modern world, bread is something we eat every day. However, good whole-grain bread is an expensive commodity. I believe many people would like to afford good bread, but end up buying cheap breads so they can feed their kids lunch every afternoon. After all, it makes fiscal sense to get three loaves of white bread instead of one loaf of heavy multi-grain slices. I agree, and I made that choice for several years.

I was raised on homemade bread. When I was growing up, it was my job to make it some of the time. When I got married, we received a bread mixer, but I only made bread when I felt like eating it hot from the oven. After all, cheap bread worked fine for sandwiches. Then my husband went back to school and we had to tighten our belts a little more. I discovered that I could make bread for less than a fourth the cost of buying it—good hearty bread, too. Plus, I could put some on the table for dinner and save money on other dinner foods.

Making bread is not the long, hard process many think. I have daughters old enough to make bread just as I did when I was young. We share the responsibility and have found that it is not that hard to make all our own bread. My daughters even make a little spending money by selling their bread. While I highly recommend a bread mixer, I did make it by hand regularly during my college years, and it's not so bad—only a few minutes more time-consuming than using the machine —which only takes ten minutes. Hand kneading is very good exercise for the arm muscles!

Bread machines, the ones that do the whole thing from start to baked, are fairly inexpensive and energy efficient. Don't worry about buying mixes for them; you can put your own ingredients in and have a hot loaf of bread every night of the week, if you choose.

Often, on a bread-making day, I make sure the rest of dinner is simple. Soups in the winter and salads in the summer are easy and go well with hot bread. That way, making bread is not an added chore; it is just part of preparing dinner.

Making our own bread allows us to try different flours and recipes, and has made me more confident when it comes to trying other breads, like pizza doughs, pitas, muffins, and pie crusts.

Remember that "bread" does not always have to mean the loaf that comes to mind first. On days when we have pancakes or waffles, I like to make a big batch so we will have leftovers. While they freeze well for another breakfast, they also make good sandwiches for lunch. Extra pancakes are an easy solution to a day I don't have bread, or the energy and time to make it.

I suppose if I felt wealthy, I might go back to buying bread, but only if I could afford the heavy whole grain kind. Homemade bread has spoiled us in that regard. Making your own bread may mean more time and energy than you want to commit. However, I encourage you to at least give it a try. It doesn't take very long, is a simple process, tastes absolutely wonderful, and saves lots (and lots) of money.

5. Think Food Groups

The world is so full of a number of things, I'm sure we should all be as happy as kings.

—Robert Louis Stevenson

The healthiest, most sustainable diet and budget regimen is one that incorporates a variety of foods in the food groups. Some of us were raised with the simple four food groups—meat, milk, fruit, and vegetables. Then the USDA Food Pyramid came out. The four food groups were slightly altered and visibly proportioned. Now we have a somewhat different and more sophisticated food and exercise guide pyramid. The government's official stand on balanced health is continually being revised and refined. It is interesting to note that in the latest version, meats have been downsized, and dried peas and beans have been added to the vegetable group, which, by the way, should make up a sizable portion of our diet.[3]

For my own purposes, I have devised simpler "food groups." There are only three—protein, fruit, and vegetables. I feel they are sufficient, well rounded health-wise, and are easy for me to comprehend and work with.

Fats, sugars, and salt are not included in my food groups. I understand that small amounts of these things are good for the body, but the fact is that they will creep into my cooking anyway. I'm not worried about getting the recommended daily amount of fats and sodium. That's already happening. Besides, fats and sugars are expensive. By cutting back on them I save money and my health.

Fruits and vegetables are two of my three food groups. While all fruits and vegetables have both vitamins and minerals, for me, fruits symbolize vitamins and vegetables symbolize minerals. It takes both to make a well-rounded meal. Keep in mind that though fruits make a nice dinner addition, they also make a great dessert. Sometimes eating something sweet at the end of a meal turns off our hunger and tells our mind we are done eating. If you like, eat your veggies for dinner and serve the fruit last.

The protein group includes meats, beans, grains, and even many vegetables. For my purposes, proteins are almost synonymous with meal fillers.

There has been some nutritional hype about "complete proteins," so I'll just interject a quick science lesson here. A protein that contains all the amino acids essential to human life is labeled "complete." These types of proteins are found mainly in meats and animal products such as eggs, milk, and cheese. Although plants contain a variety of amino acids, only a few plant sources provide the complete array in a single plant. That doesn't mean a diet needs meat to provide enough nutrition; it just means we need a variety of plant foods. Beans and grains are good healthy sources of all necessary amino acids.

Meat is expensive. If your goal is to eat for less money, meat should be considered optional. Most meals can be satisfying while using less meat than the recipe calls for. In some recipes it can be left out altogether. Baked beans, stir-fry, even chicken soup work well by adding a little bouillon instead of meat. If using meat, try adding half the amount called for. In meatballs and meatloaf, you can use less hamburger and more oatmeal without drastically changing the texture or taste.

Sometimes our desire for meat at a meal is psychological. Some people feel they don't have a complete meal if it doesn't contain some visible meat. Use these tricks for cutting back meat until you learn to mentally feel full on beans or rice.

There are plenty of good proteins in beans and whole grains to satisfy your body's nutritional needs. A meal based on one of the four main fillers and rounded out with fruits and vegetables will provide good balanced nutrition for your family at a low cost.

6. Presentation Is Everything

Creativity is a lot like looking at the world through a kaleidoscope. You look at a set of elements, the same ones that everyone else sees, but then reassemble those floating bits and pieces into an enticing new possibility.

—Rosabeth Moss Kanter

The way food is presented at mealtime can influence how much of that food will be eaten. Food that needs to be used quickly before going bad can be presented in a manner that will make it particularly appealing to your family. Conversely, food of which you have little, or that you want to conserve, can be presented to look like enough. Nutrition is important, and we want our families to be full and feel satisfied, but we have already established that most of us eat more than we need to. The chef is like a magician, and food presentation can be considered the smoke and mirrors of the magic act. Those eating the meal feel full, well fed, and satisfied, but are actually eating what you want them to in the proportions you decide. You can focus your diners' attention on the basic fillers and at the same time make the meal feel sumptuous. Presentation is a great way to use less food or make it stretch, thereby stretching your money as well.

Whole to Parts

If I put a bowl of whole apples on the table for dessert, everyone will eat one. However, if I serve two or three apples in slices, everyone eats as much as he or she wants, and I usually have a few slices left over. This works for any kind of fruit. Since fresh fruit is fairly expensive, I usually serve it cut up. Even a little fills out a meal or makes a good dessert.

Single Servings

Sometimes I have lots of little bits of leftovers—not enough to feed everyone, but enough that the fridge desperately needs to be cleaned out. On those nights we have a "smorgasbord" dinner. I warm it all up, and put a spoonful of each leftover on every plate. The kids may not understand limiting their serving to just a spoonful if we passed the leftovers at the table, but will be satisfied with a plate already served with four or five different leftovers. Everyone gets plenty to eat, and if anyone wants more, there is usually still something he or she can have.

I follow the same principle for yogurt. When the little cups go on sale, I can get them for the same price per ounce as the big tubs. I buy a few different flavors, and put a heaping spoonful of two or three flavors on every plate for breakfast. Everyone feels they are getting a great treat with their toast (because there are multiple flavors instead of one), and as a family we use only a few cups of yogurt instead of a full six or eight ounce cup for each person.

Dress Up Or Down

Obviously, how a dish tastes can determine how much is eaten. We want our families to enjoy their meals, and no one would purposely put a bad-tasting dish on the table. However, a good cook can tweak taste just enough to make a dish extra tasty or not so much. For example, if carrots are going to be the vegetable of our meal, and I have only a few left, I can put out carrot sticks or steam them with a little salt, and my family will eat and enjoy them, but not in excess. On the other hand, if I have logs of carrots and I need to fill out a meal, I will make basil carrots—one of our favorites—and my kids will eat more carrots. Lettuce served plain and passed with dressing is a nice side vegetable, but included in a taco salad or salad bar make it a main dish. If we have lettuce just starting to turn brown, I often add a can of tuna and a little mayonnaise, which guarantees it will be gone that meal. If I serve baked potatoes, we use half as many as when I serve them mashed - plus we save ourselves butter, milk, and gravy. Not that we never have mashed potatoes. We just save them for a special meal. Fruit salad, also a family favorite, is saved for times when I have plenty of a variety of fruits. Otherwise, we eat fruit sliced on a plate.

In the summer, when vegetables are plentiful, and we feel less like hot and heavy fillers, I like to make our veggie dishes more fun and exciting than usual so my children get enough to eat even in warm weather.

This trick also works well when I notice sickness coming on in our house. I can dress up chicken soup or turn juices into warm cider to encourage eating or drinking that item.

One Dish Separately

Several components to a meal always make the table look fuller and seem like more. One dish meals can be wonderful in their place, but if you are stretching a meal, try breaking it up. As an example, spaghetti looks much grander if served in separate bowls of sauce, noodles, and Parmesan cheese, rather than combined in a casserole. Consider putting on the makings for tacos and keeping the enchiladas for special occasions. Serve hash browns and eggs instead of a breakfast casserole.

Always think about the food you have and what you want the meal to accomplish. You are the magician in charge. Dress up, dress down, single serve, separate, and combine foods to use what you have. Be a master presenter and save money!

7. Buying Bulk

Wisdom is the principle thing; therefore get wisdom;
and with all thy getting get understanding.

—Proverbs 4:7

We have all heard that buying food in bulk saves us money. It certainly can, but here again is the big industry feeding the public with over-generalized half-truths. There are a few principles to remember when buying bulk.

Unit Cost

Calculate cost! If you need to, take a calculator to the store with you to figure out which size is really best. Many stores do that for you on the shelf price label. Look for the small print that tells how much you are paying per ounce or single unit. You can then compare different sizes accordingly. Should you buy raisins in the individual boxes, the small canister, or the big bag? You can also calculate the cost of different brands this way. Sometimes two brands will put products in different-sized containers. By figuring out the unit price you can decide which is giving you a better bargain. You may be surprised at how often the bigger package is more expensive per unit than the smaller.

In general, staple foods like flour, sugar, beans, and so forth, are cheaper in bulk. There are exceptions, however. At the store where I buy my sugar, the price per pound is the same regardless of the size I buy. Since I'm paying the same price per pound, my next consideration is convenience. I like working with smaller bags, and they fit better in my kitchen space, so I buy sugar in ten pound bags instead of big twenty-five or fifty pound bags. Sometimes the five-pound bags of flour go on sale for less per pound than a bigger bag. Stay current on price per unit and you will know a good deal when you see it.

Storage Cost

Consider storage and ease of use. A gigantic container of mustard may save lots of money, but do you want to sacrifice that much fridge space for several months, and will you use it all before it goes bad? Are you willing to refill your smaller container at the savings of a few cents?

Some things can be bought in bulk and portioned out for storage. A big #10 can of enchilada sauce is considerably cheaper than several smaller cans. It can be portioned into using sizes and frozen in zippered sandwich bags. Buy hamburger in bulk and freeze it in dinner-sized portions for later. Make sure to figure in the cost of your own packaging and storing.

Club Membership Cost

Decide if your club membership to stores that specialize in bulk products is worth it. If you use several things from that store, than it is probably a good deal. On the other hand, they often sell name brand foods, and you may be able to buy a store brand for less at your local grocer.

We looked into a membership at a bulk foods store once. I went with a friend who had a membership and wrote down the sizes and costs of items we used. At home I compared those prices and sizes with those at my regular store. We calculated how much we would save and then added the cost of membership to it. We came out exactly even. So we decided to try a membership for a year and see if it was worth it. I found that I didn't get there as often as I had thought I would. It wasn't as close and convenient as our regular store. When I went, I spent more than I had intended on things we would normally have done without. I also learned an important lesson about container size, which is the next principle. Plus, I noticed that regular grocery store sales prices were almost always better deals than the bulk store prices—which never went on sale. Although I miss browsing that store, we no longer have a membership there.

Usage Cost

At the bulk store, frozen orange juice cans came in a larger size—not the twelve-ounce can I normally used. However, they were less expensive per ounce, so I bought some. I discovered that we still used one can for every two breakfasts, the same as when we used the smaller can. Because it was reconstituted and in the pitcher, we just drank more orange juice. I was actually spending more money per meal on orange juice than before. Sure, we had more juice in our diet, but it wasn't really a noticeable amount and certainly not necessary.

I learned that just saving per ounce was not always saving overall. I have since become more watchful of foods we may eat purely because they are open or available. I bought a twelve pound bag of chocolate chips at the bulk store and found that we had chocolate chip cookies much more often, and usually on a whim instead of for a purpose—an unnecessary waste of several ingredients. Sometimes I buy the smaller container, even if it may not be the absolute best deal per unit. We simply do not need the larger quantity, and I can save money in the long run.

Serving Cost

Stores are full of convenient single-serving items. It looks so easy to buy, and many people do not think about how much they are spending on the packaging. For example, cheese sticks are a popular kid snack, but how hard is it to get a block of bulk cheese and take two minutes to cut it into sticks and put them in snack bags or plastic wrap? The same could be done with applesauce, fruit cocktail, chips, and juice. Making your own single serve portions can save you lots of dollars and save the world a landfill as well.

Our daughters came home from school one day after an intensive presentation about recycling. They wanted to know why we didn't recycle more things. We explained that we believed recycling was important, but that our lifestyle also promoted using less packaging initially. As a family of eight we used, and rarely filled, the smallest size of garbage can offered by the city. We didn't take the newspaper, and used their old school papers as scratch paper at home. We conscientiously bought food that had little packaging. After discussing what items they had learned should be recycled, they came to the realization that we didn't use many of those things in our house. While recycling is important, it is even better for the environment not to need that packaging in the first place.

8. Eat with the Seasons

*Behold, I have given you every herb bearing seed,
which is upon the face of all the earth, and every tree, in
the which is the fruit of a tree yielding seed; to you it shall
be for meat.*

—Genesis 1:29

We all know watermelon and nuts are seasonal. Did you know bananas are, too? Anticipating sale prices and planning your menu around those products can save you lots of money. Plan for cabbage and potato dishes around St. Patrick's Day when those items go on sale. Mexican foods like rice, beans, taco toppings, and tortillas are a good choice when they go on sale for Cinco de Mayo. Stock up on hot dogs for the year around the Fourth of July. Sweet potatoes and cranberries (cranberries freeze well) are least expensive in November. Baking items go on sale for the holidays, so that's a good time to purchase extra flour, sugars, canned milk, baking powder, and some spices.

Many grocery stores have annual or semi-annual case lot sales—often in January or August or both. Ask you local stores if they have one and plan for it. Buy when things are less expensive and wait for a sale to replenish used items. For example, I don't add green beans to my grocery list every time I use a can. I know I'll probably be able to buy a whole case at a great price in August, so I keep mental track of how many cans I have left since my last purchase, and use them sparingly to make them last until the next big sale.

Fresh fruits and vegetables are usually versatile in meals, so buy the least expensive types available in a given season. We eat lots of apples, oranges, and bananas in the winter months. Peaches, plums, cherries, and so forth, are treats for the summer months when they are in season. Squash, mushrooms, avocados, and tomatoes all have a season, too.

Keep in mind that advertising doesn't necessarily mean something is a good deal. Some "summer" produce gets advertised in the winter when the supermarket ships it from South America. Compare price per pound and you may find that regular unadvertised apples and oranges are still a better choice.

Many grocery stores have a bargain spot where you can get produce and other items at clearance prices. I get many of my best deals here and then change my menu accordingly. Make sure that what you are getting is really a deal, though. I once bought a case of strawberries at a clearance price and discovered, after throwing away half because they were spoiled, that I had, in essence, paid full price for the good ones.

Plan your menu around shopping ads. Many ads are available on-line. It might help to keep a simple log of sale prices and dates. A year or two of observant shopping will alert you to seasons so you can plan your menu around sales.

9. Drinks

In character, in manner, in style, in all things, the supreme excellence is simplicity.

—Henry Wadsworth Longfellow

We've all heard that we should drink six to eight glasses of water a day. How many glasses of water do you really drink each day? How many glasses of something else do you drink every day? How much do you pay for the other liquids that you drink every day? Most of us could help our food budget dramatically simply by changing what we drink.

Let's start with water. Thirty years ago the idea to market bottled water seemed crazy—like the muppet on Sesame Street who was always trying to sell air for a nickel from his overcoat's inside pocket. Who would pay for something that was free anytime from the tap? Today bottled water is big business. Many think it is healthier than tap water. Here, again, is advertising at work. The Federal Drug Administration regulates bottled water, while city water is regulated by the Environmental Protection Agency. Incidentally, the EPA's standards for water are more stringent than the FDA's. City water is highly monitored, while bottled water is rarely policed. In one city we lived in, we got an annual report in the mail detailing the specifications and how our city's water measured up. It included parts per million of minerals and any contaminants. Bottled water labels have very little information for the consumer.[4]

Companies who sell filters and bottled water want us to know that there is nothing bad in their water. They neglect to tell us that they have taken out many of the trace minerals that are good for us. Only recently have some companies advertised bottled waters with minerals and vitamins added. It's like our society switched from whole wheat to white flour that is now being enriched.

Americans can spend more than a thousand times more money per gallon on bottled water as compared to tap water.[5] Drink tap water and save big bucks.

Consider the other drinks you ingest. Many are high calorie, high cost, and low nutrition. Soda, coffee, punch, even juices are not the optimal nutritional bang for your buck. Try drinking water with lunch and dinner. Water is not only healthy but also can satiate hunger pangs. We keep cups at all the sinks in our home to encourage our children to drink water when they are thirsty from playing hard. We also fill all the glasses at the dinner table before dinner to encourage adequate water intake during mealtime.

There are a few tricks we have tried to make our drink dollar stretch even more.

- We drink juice only at breakfast. I buy frozen concentrate juices and then add one more can of water than the packaging calls for. The taste difference is minimal and I get an extra couple of glasses of juice out of each can.

- Milk is something we usually use only on cereal. We eat other foods high in calcium to make sure we get enough of that mineral. Orange juice and even apple juice can be bought supplemented with calcium for no extra money. My family is used to drinking 1% milk. Sometimes I find whole milk or 2% milk for the same price or only a few cents more than 1% milk. If I buy milk with a higher fat content than what we normally drink, I can add water and get up to a gallon and a quart for the price of a gallon.

Changing what your family drinks might be very difficult, not just because of the sugar and caffeine, but because drinking is very habitual. We are used to drinking certain things at certain times of the day—juice for breakfast, soda while we drive or watch TV. Many people carry around a water bottle almost all day long. We drink at meetings and recreational activities and social gatherings. We are so used to having something continually on hand ready to drink, that for many of us it has become a habit of comfort more than necessity. Keep in mind what and when you drink, and see if you can modify habits to save money without losing nutrition.

10. Convenience

Individuality is the salt of common life. You may
have to live in a crowd but you do not have to live like it,
nor subsist on its food.

—Henry Van Dyke

We pay for convenience. Zippered plastic bags, muffin tin liners, dishwashers, and paper towels are all great inventions. Keeping our lives simple and handy seems to be the desire of almost every company with an advertising budget. Next to the country magazine article about the family farm is a full-page spread about the latest and greatest dishwasher pellets. New products show up all the time. How did we possibly live without them?

Notice the price and really evaluate whether a convenience item is worth that much to you. Dishwasher pellets are much more expensive than regular liquid dish soap—not to mention the savings in water and energy if you wash your dishes by hand. The latest in mopping technology is nice, but are your floors getting ten dollars worth cleaner? Do you really need the name brand triple zippered freezer protection baggies, or do regular fold-over baggies work just fine for most of your needs? The "stronger" paper towels are three times as expensive as the regular kind. You could use three cheap paper towels for the same price.

Consider the disposable things you use every day. Is there a substitute? Grease pans instead of using muffin liners. Use a rag and launder it instead of reaching for the paper towels.

Watch how you use disposable items and see if there is a better way. Use plastic snap lid containers for leftovers instead of plastic wrap. Use plastic wrap instead of sandwich baggies. Use fold-over sandwich baggies instead of zippered bags. In other words, try finding a cheaper solution so you can spend less money on non-food items.

I will be the first to admit that convenience is nice. You will have to decide what conveniences are worth what price to you. Just realize that companies are not really looking out for your welfare; they are trying to sell you a product so they can make money. Take charge of your vulnerability and your money.

11. Preserve! Preserve! Preserve!

Be studious in your profession, and you will be learned. Be industrious and frugal, and you will be rich. Be sober and temperate, and you will be healthy. Be in general virtuous, and you will be happy. At least you will, by such conduct, stand the best chance of such consequences.

—Benjamin Franklin

Preserving foods—canning, freezing, jamming, and so on—seems to be an art of the past. People who have never preserved their own food may consider canning, freezing, or drying to be complicated and time-consuming processes. The fact is that most food preservation techniques take about as much know-how as making pancakes. Some preservation does take time, but much does not. All food-preserving processes are logical and simple, and you can decide whether the effort involved in any particular project is worth the money you might save.

Look for Free or Inexpensive

I have found that, in general, only free or very inexpensive foods are cost effective to preserve. You will probably not save money on applesauce by buying a box of apples and saucing them yourself. However, if neighbor Joe has an apple tree full of apples he does not want, you may be able to have delicious homemade applesauce for the year. Most people who do not use much or any of their fruit are thrilled to have someone pick and use it. Offering a jar of whatever you made with the fruit as a "thank you" will ensure good relations and probably guarantee

27

an invitation to harvest the fruit again the next year.

We happen to live close to areas where we can pick wild berries—serviceberries, chokecherries, and huckleberries—for jamming. It is a fun family experience, not to mention easy on the pocketbook.

Once in a great while I find a deal at the store. For example, sometimes I can find an entire forty-pound case of overripe but still decent bananas for four dollars. Homemade dried bananas are my kids' all-time favorite treat. Invariably, another customer will ask, "What are you going to do with *all* those bananas?" Then I counter with, "Have you ever tasted homemade dried bananas? They are better than candy!" Also, bananas can easily be thrown in the freezer whole, to be used later in banana breads, cakes or muffins.

Take Advantage of Opportunity

When it comes to food preservation, you have to go with the flow. Every year will offer different options. To be cost efficient, you have to jump at every possible opportunity, be flexible, and be willing to try new things. Some years I have canned jar after jar of apricots; the next year there may be no apricot harvest. I may find a great strawberry deal at the store one day and need to spend the next day making jam. Once some friends gave us several zucchini squashes that we couldn't eat fast enough. We spent an evening grating and freezing the rest for bread later in the year.

Invest in the Right Tools

A small investment in preserving essentials will save you money in the long run.

For Jams and Jellies

Making jams and jellies requires only a few small jars, a big pot, and pectin. Pectin can be fairly expensive, but usually goes on sale in the spring when strawberries come on. Stock up then, and you will save money and be able to make apple jellies and marmalade in the fall and winter. Jars are plentiful and cheap at second hand stores. Let people know you are looking. Many are happy to find someone who can use empty jars. Freezer jams don't require jars at all—only a plastic container with a lid.

If you want your jams and jellies on the shelf instead of in the freezer, a canner will be helpful. Some experts recommend processing jams in a water bath canner. However, if you are going to use your jams and jellies in a few months, some easier tricks from our foremothers will do. Melted paraffin poured one-fourth to one-half an inch thick directly on top of the jam before the lid is put on will create a good seal. Personally, I like to use new canning lids, so just after I've poured the boiling jam in the jars, I screw the lids on firmly and turn the jars upside down for five to ten minutes. This gets the rubber on the lids hot and soft. Then I turn them right side up and the cooling jam contracts and seals the lids on. You know a jar is sealed when you can push on the lid and it does not pop up and down.

Canner

A canner is an inexpensive investment and nice to have on hand. There are two kinds—water bath canners and steam canners. I like a steam canner because it is faster and easier for me. However, many experts recommend water bath canners because steam canners have not been conclusively tested to know whether the fruit gets to the proper temperature for the required time to kill bacteria. I have heard of some steam canner users who make up for this shortcoming by lengthening the cooking time. Others choose to be safe rather than sorry, and use only water bath canners. There are people who use steam for some foods and water bath for others. If you choose to jump into the canning world, talk to several people with experience, check out some good books, and do a little product research before spending money.

Dehydrator

A dehydrator is a more expensive food-preserving item but will pay for itself fairly quickly. I spent forty dollars on my first dehydrator. I used it for several years even though it did not dry the food evenly and required constant tending and tray rotation. I eventually found a good dehydrator on sale for $150. It heats evenly and has different settings for different foods.

Many foods can be dried. I dry mostly fruit. Almost all the snacks my children eat are fruits we dried ourselves. Dehydrators are a great way for kids to be involved. They can lay fruit out on the trays, check to see if it's done, and bag the fruit when it's dry. Plus, they get an appreciation for the work that goes into an easy snack.

If you want to get fancy, a dehydrator can make homemade jerky, fruit leather, and seasoned veggie chips as well as dried fruit—all healthy and fun to try.

Freezer

Invest in a freezer. It doesn't have to be expensive. Our first freezer was a freebie; a friend had owned it for twenty years and didn't want it anymore. When we moved, we left it behind and searched the classified ads in our new location. Sure enough, there were plenty of old freezers for sale—most under $50.

I prefer an upright freezer to a chest freezer. It takes up less space in the garage, and more important, it lets me see and easily access everything.

A freezer in the garage allows you to stock up on good deals, store the freezer jam you made from all those strawberries, gives you a place for extra meals when you double the casserole recipe, and lets you have emergency food for disaster preparedness.

Freezer space should be organized, both for efficiency and hygienic food-handling purposes. Meats, juices, fruits, veggies, and jams should all have their own shelf or space. There are basically two ways to organize your freezer space. If your big freezer is easily accessible, you can use your fridge freezer just like an extra shelf for all of your juices or jams. Or you can treat your fridge freezer like a mini big one, and stock it with a little of everything and replenish from the outdoor one when you run low on anything.

Many foods lend themselves well to freezing. Dairy products generally freeze well. You can stock up on a good deal at the store and put hard cheeses, cottage cheese, yogurt, butter, even milk in the freezer for later. Remember that milk will expand when frozen, so drink a glass to leave room in the carton for the rest to expand as it freezes.

Peaches are delicious frozen. Peel and slice them into quart sized bags and you have a perfect waffle topping or ready peach pie filling. Pumpkins and zucchini seem to be plentiful in the fall. Grate the zucchini and freeze it for zucchini bread later. Pumpkins can be baked whole. When cool, peel and take out seeds. Mash pulp and freeze in quart sized zipper bags. You can have pumpkin muffins or cookies in March if you want.

Apples, apricots, peaches, berries, tomatoes, corn, and squashes are often surplus and all of them preserve well.

Double the Recipe

We all have days we don't feel like even looking at our kitchen. We postpone thinking about dinner until the last possible moment. Maybe we have a super busy day and just don't have time to spend even thirty minutes on a meal. Don't break down and give in to fast food and expensive prepared dishes. With a little forethought, there is a solution.

Double everything you cook. Make two pans of lasagna for dinner instead of one. It's not that much extra effort, and it actually saves resources like hot water, dishwashing soap, energy used to cook, and maybe even ingredients, like butter used for sautéing onions. Cover the extra casserole with a layer of plastic wrap and then foil so it will keep well, and put it in the freezer. Remember to label it and write the date on it. Now you have an instant meal!

Soups double easily and can go in a gallon sized zippered bag for easy freezing. Make sure to lay it flat so it will stack in the freezer nicely and thaw quickly.

Keep a shelf in the freezer designated for frozen meals. In the morning on one of those no time or no desire days, just pull out a meal and set it on the counter to defrost for the day.

Need a dessert but don't have time to make it? Almost all cookies freeze well and defrost quickly. Cookie dough and pie dough also freeze well. I keep a batch of sugar cookie dough in my fridge freezer so I can quickly make cookie shapes for different holidays.

Freezer meals and desserts make great presents, too. A meal is an easy and much appreciated gift for someone who just had a baby or family emergency. A freezer meal also makes a great "Thinking of You" gift for a busy family.

12. Snacks

*One of life's greatest paradoxes is that nearly every-
one wants to improve his circumstances but hardly anyone
wants to improve himself.*

—Milton Sills

Snacks are part of the culture of America—a largely unnecessary one, I might add. Most cultures do not eat between meals. Two or three meals a day are plenty for the majority of adults and children. Obviously, babies need to eat more often during the day, but even toddlers can make it between meals without snacking. In fact, recent research suggests that eating less than the average American could lead to a longer life.[6]

Hilaire Belloc wrote:

> The Vulture eats between his meals,
> And that's the reason why
> He very, very rarely feels
> As well as you or I.
> His eye is dull, his head is bald,
> His neck is growing thinner.
> Oh, what a lesson for us all
> To only eat at dinner.[7]

Children are much better and much heartier eaters at dinner if they are hungry. Hunger is not a bad thing. It is a natural, physical desire, and we don't need to be afraid of it. Eating when we *should* instead of when we *want* to shows self-control—something our society seems to have lost in many aspects. Our bodies are creatures of habit. When accustomed snacks are regularly denied, the hunger pangs do not come as often and are not as mind consuming as before. Snacking in the evening is a habit I have broken more than once. The first two days are the hardest. After that, I realize I feel better both in the evening and the morning, and I sleep better, too. Get rid of snacks, and you will save hundreds of dollars a year.

If you absolutely need something, or feel your child does, to make it to the next meal, keep two rules in mind. First, snacks are not intended to fill you up. This is not a meal. An apple or a handful of nuts or a piece of bread is adequate. Second, keep it healthy and inexpensive. Healthy snacks will not depress your appetite for dinner as much as fat and sugar will. Unhealthy snacks are some of the most expensive foods you can buy. Chips, soft drinks, cookies, fruit snacks, even flavored yogurt and granola bars are all high in sugar, salt, and cost. Evaluate how much you have been spending on snack foods every month. Be honest with yourself, and you'll likely be amazed at how much you could save by giving up unnecessary and unhealthy snacks.

13. Picky Eaters

Self-respect is at the bottom of all good manners. They are the expression of discipline, of good-will, of respect for other people's rights and comfort and feelings.

—Edward S. Martin

Kids who are picky eaters often cost their families extra food money. Parents, who understandably want their children to eat and get the right amount of nutrition, sometimes buy "what my kids will eat." Consumer marketing uses campaign slogans like "Has a full serving of fruit" or "Kids love it" to get parents to buy expensive new things. While the advertising may be true, these foods—cheese sticks, fruit bars, cereal bars, and fruit leather—are also usually full of sugars, salt, and preservatives. Plus, they are often individually wrapped and sporting a picture of a popular toy or TV figure. Parents pay a lot for expensive and colorful packaging because it is enticing to their children.

Here's the thing—kids in third world countries don't starve to death because they don't like their beans and rice. Children are usually only as picky as their parents will allow. In fact, often a picky child has a picky parent.

Appreciation of food served and the effort behind the dish at the table should be learned young. We all have preferences and different taste in food, but that doesn't mean we can't eat well-prepared food that's served to us. We all have different opinions about apparel and home décor, but that doesn't mean we turn up our noses and refuse to walk into our neighbor's house just because we don't like her window treatments. Besides, any adult knows that taste buds change with age. Trying and re-trying foods we may not like gives our taste buds a chance to learn to like something later in life. At the very least, learning to eat things we don't like teaches us tolerance and good manners.

I already discussed our family's change from white to brown rice. Some foods become more tolerable with gradual inclusion. Often with children, however, pickiness is just a matter of appreciation.

After baby number three came along, I got into the cold cereal habit. I really like cold cereal, and enjoyed the daily breakfast treat. Our kids enjoyed it as well, at first, but soon started arguing over favorites and whining if we were out of certain cereals. The attitudes at breakfast seemed to carry over to mealtimes in general. The kids became very vocal about things that didn't appeal to them or what they wished we were eating instead. I recognized the gradual change for the worse but couldn't think of a reason for the behavior.

One evening at dinner, out of sheer frustration, my husband announced to our children that we would be serving oatmeal for breakfast every day until they started appreciating what was served. At the moment, I didn't understand how he thought changing breakfast would affect dinner behavior. The first few oatmeal days were miserable, but we stuck with it. Unfinished bowls of oatmeal were served cold at lunchtime before lunch could be eaten. After only a week, not only had the complaining stopped at all meals, but the kids had also learned to eat and enjoy oatmeal. We were amazed at the simple solution to a general problem of pickiness—and no one starved to death!

Since that learning episode, I have made it a policy to keep breakfast and lunch simple so our kids look forward to and appreciate dinner and other "treat" meals. My husband and I also make it a point at meals to show gratitude ourselves for the food with which we are blessed and for the effort made in its preparation.

This principle holds true in many aspects of child rearing. Overindulgence leads to dissatisfaction with life in general. Those who appreciate and enjoy life with gratitude have been fed metaphorically on simplicity and have been disciplined to deal with what life hands them.

14. Grow Your Own

While having a garden . . . is often useful in reducing food costs and making available delicious fresh fruits and vegetables, it does much more than this. Who can gauge the value of that special chat between daughter and Dad as they weed or water the garden? How do we evaluate the good that comes from the obvious lessons of planting, cultivating, and the eternal law of the harvest?

—Spencer W. Kimball

Gardening is a great way to save money on your food bill and enjoy better-tasting fruits and vegetables. Our first home had plenty of yard space for a garden and several mature fruit trees. We thoroughly enjoyed trying out new plant varieties and gardening techniques every year. The kids loved to munch on peas, cherry tomatoes, apricots, plums, and apples while they played outside. My husband and I enjoyed eating lots of delicious fresh fruits and vegetables so cheaply.

Now we live in an apartment with no gardening options. I cringe when I pay good money for expensive but bland-tasting vegetables at the grocery store. I do keep an outdoor container of common herbs by the kitchen door in the summer for grilling and cooking.

If you have any yard at all, devote some space to growing food. You don't have to be a "gardener-type" to be successful at getting a few tomatoes for summer eating. A large garden gives you the option of trying lots of things, but even a little plot or container can produce enough food to put several dollars back in your pocketbook. Although I have gardened for a few years, I am continually amazed at how much can be produced from just a little bit of dirt.

15. Menus and Grocery Lists

What we hope ever to do with ease, we must learn first to do with diligence.

—Samuel Johnson

A dollar will stretch a lot with a little planning and organization. Most people will agree with the obvious, that planning ahead means you will visit the store less often, which saves money both in gas and spur of the moment spending.

Only four sheets of lined paper are needed for food budget bookkeeping each month. There are no complicated forms to make or copy. I use regular notebook paper—the kind you can buy for a few cents a package when school supplies go on sale in the summer. All four pages are kept in a magnetic clip on my fridge for easy access and marking. They are the Running List, Menu, Master List, and Budget.

Running List

A running list is simply a designated spot where you write down what you need when you think of it. I find it nearly impossible to sit down once a month to make a grocery list and remember absolutely every household item I need. A lined piece of paper on the fridge with a handy pen or pencil gives me a place to jot things down during the month. If I notice that I'm low on vanilla while I'm making cookies, I can immediately pause, write it on my list, and continue my baking. Without a running list, I find that even with the best-planned menus and master lists, I am driving all month to stores for one or two items I forgot I needed.

Sample List:

Milk
Eggs
Flour
Toothpaste
Plain yogurt
Vanilla
Pinto beans

Menu

The menu is simply a blank calendar-type page with the meals set out for the month. Since I designate a basic food for each day of the week, I can easily fill in dinners for each weeknight (such as rice dishes, bean dishes, potato dishes, and so on). Here is a sample (remember, Saturdays are Left Overs days):

Sunday	Monday (noodles)	Tuesday (rice)	Wednesday (beans)	Thursday (potatoes)	Friday (grain)
Sweet & Sour	Spaghetti	Stir-fry	Chili	Baked Potato Bar	Creamed Eggs on Toast
Porcupine Meatballs	Stroganoff	Rice soup	Tacos/ Refried Beans	Hot Potato Salad	Scones
Stew	Pasta Salad	Curry	Hamburger Pie	Clam Chowder	Navajo Tacos
Homemade Egg Rolls	Lasagna	Missionary Rice	Lentil Soup	Mashed Potatoes & Gravy	Waffles
Biscuits & Gravy	Tuna Noodle Casserole	Fried Rice	Baked Beans	Scalloped Potatoes	Spoon Bread

Once in a while, I find I have an opportunity to go shopping, but don't have time to sit down and make up a formal menu for the month.

I keep a list of meal options on the fridge. I divide the page into categories like "Breakfasts," "Rice," "Beans," "Potatoes," and so on. For shopping, I can easily go down the list and make sure I have the items necessary to fix at least thirty of those meals. Then, as I make the meal, I cross it off.

Each menu method has its advantages. The disadvantage of the list method is that because meals are not designated to a certain day, I often make the ones I like best, or that are easiest, first. It's nice to have these treat meals spread out through the calendar month.

Breakfasts and lunches are not on the menu because they are already pretty much planned. Lunches are peanut butter and jam sandwiches and fruit or leftovers. Breakfasts rotate through oatmeal, rice, toast, and eggs. I just make sure I put those items on the grocery list every month.

Master List

The master list is my grocery list. I sit down before the beginning of the month with my running list, my menu, and a sheet for the master list. On the master list page I head several columns with names of stores I will go to during the month. Then I write down each item on my running list under the name of the store from which I will buy it. Next, I go through the menu and write down items needed for meals for the next month from each store. When everything is written down that is needed for the month, I estimate what each item will cost. I write down the estimated amount next to that item. Then I total the amount I estimate I will spend at each store. I make a grand total estimate of everything we will buy for the month. If my grand total exceeds my budget for the month, I may have to re-evaluate the menu.

It is important when making the master list to remember that you won't be able to buy everything for the month at the beginning of that month. For example, I write down how many gallons of milk I will need, but I will have to buy them throughout the month. Make sure you plan and save enough money to buy your perishables as you use them. It is also a good idea to plan extra money to spend on unexpected deals. You may get to the store and find that case of bananas for four dollars, or a super deal on tortillas or tomato sauce. Staying in budget requires making allowances for great deals or going without them.

Cross items off your list as you buy them. It may also be helpful to write down the actual cost of some items so you have a better estimate next time.

Example:

Walmart	$	Town & Country	$	Smith's	$
Salt-3	1	Potatoes	5	Cheese	6
Flour	9	Lettuce	2	Milk	4
Margarine-4	4	Carrots	3	Fruit?	5
Vanilla	2	Misc. veggies	5	Eggs-5	7
Toothpaste	3	Fruit?	5		
Plain yogurt	2	Pinto beans	12		
Total	21	Total	32	Total	22

Budget

The budget page is what makes you feel good about yourself and helps you keep track of your spending. At the top write "Food Budget for (Month)" and the amount you are going to spend on food. As you shop, write down the amount you spend (to the penny with no rounding!) and the store at which you spent it. You will be able to monitor your spending as you compare your master list and your actual budget amounts. There have been months I have run out of money before the month was out. Usually, it is because I have chosen a great deal over some items on my list. The challenge then is to revise the menu and use what I have in the house. We have sometimes gone without milk or used stored powdered milk for a week or two until the new month.

Learning to make do at the end of the month may sound like poor budgeting. It may be, but it can also be a great learning experience. Many of us think we don't have anything to eat when our cupboards are actually full. Requiring ourselves to stay in the budget and live with what we have on hand is a good way to get the creative juices flowing. A can of cranberry sauce doesn't have to wait for turkey; it can be served as the fruit of almost any meal. Bags with little bits of frozen veggies mix well to make enough for a dinner. Some of my best recipes were developed during "make do" days. At the least, your kids will probably have fond memories of some odd meal concoction to tell the grandkids.

On the other hand, when you have a little excess at the end of the month, it is a time to celebrate. Splurge on something with the last little bit. You have earned it.

There is nothing to compare with the feeling of pride and accomplishment when I stay in the budget and feed my family well.

Example:

April Food Budget = 200.00		
	Amount spent @ each store	Total amount spent
Town & Country	36.12	36.12
Smith's	52.34	88.46
Jo-Ann's (buttons)	2.16	90.62
Walmart	65.89	156.51
Grand Total		**156.51**

16. Do Unto Others

What the world lacks most today is men who occupy themselves with the needs of other men. In this unselfish labor a blessing falls on both the helper and the helped.

—Albert Schweitzer

We all reach points in our life when we cannot do for ourselves what needs to be done. We must necessarily rely on others to help us—emotionally, financially, socially, and so forth. I have found in my life a principle I believe is crucial in money management as well as other aspects of existence.

The Bible says "Do unto others as you would have others do unto you." Religious or not, I think most people agree that treating others how we want to be treated is a good rule of thumb. If we are generous with what we have, others will be willing to help us out of a pinch.

Lloyd C. Douglas wrote a popular classic novel published in 1929 called *Magnificent Obsession*. The main character in the story is obsessed with doing secret kindnesses and documenting how the universe seems to repay him.

I've seen this basic principle play out in our situation time and again. When I am willing to take a meal to someone who is sick, tend another family's children, make an effort to be a good neighbor, or spend time for my church and community, I find that others reach out to me unasked. We have answered our door many times to find someone with extra produce, nice second-hand clothes, even complete meals "just because."

Generosity also brings satisfaction. When we are selfish, we become unhappy with what we have. Giving what we can automatically instills gratitude and serenity with our lot in life.

At my church, we are encouraged to fast once a month for two consecutive meals. We then donate the money we would normally spend on those skipped meals, and our donation is used to feed those who have nothing. Though we live frugally, our fasting helps us recognize that there are others with less, and makes us grateful for our resources and ability to help someone else.

Stretching your grocery dollar to the fullest requires generosity. Note that generosity is not stupidity. There is often a fine line between sacrifice and generosity and plain ridiculous stupidity. Each situation is different and demands evaluation. The principle here is that if you will help out others in need of what you can give, you will find help when you need it as well. What goes around comes around.

17. Conclusion

The highest reward for man's toil is not what he gets for it, but what he becomes by it.

—John Ruskin

Now that you know what to do, take Nike's advice and DO IT! Really try. Here are some points to help you stay motivated:

Keep your budget and goal posted on your fridge so it is always in your mind.

Stay on top. Plan the month so you won't get bogged down emotionally or financially half-way through. Write down what you spent the minute you get home from shopping. Start in the morning with a good, inexpensive breakfast and know what needs to be done for dinner so you are not stuck deciding what to make a few minutes before serving time. Think ahead and make sure your menu matches whatever else has to be done each day.

Watch for other ways to save money around the house. Shake out the tablecloth and flip it over instead of laundering it after every meal. Use dryer sheets more than once or cut them in half. They will last through at least two loads. Static is higher in winter and lower in summer. Maybe you can stop using dyer sheets altogether in the summer. Watch toilet paper usage and teach your kids how much is necessary. Facial tissue is often on sale in the fall for school—a good time to stock up. Wash your dishes by hand instead of using the dishwasher every day. I discovered, after a few years of keeping track, that feeding our kids a daily vitamin cut down on the money we spent each winter for cold medicines, doctor's visits, and tissues. Besides the money savings, we knew our kids were getting ample vitamins and minerals.

Keep frugality fun. Some meals are too involved to make routinely, but can be a great family activity and learning experience. Try making your own tortillas, fried chicken, French fries, noodles, pitas, bagels, or ravioli. There's huge satisfaction in knowing you know how, even if you don't want to make a weekly habit of it.

Involve your children. The before-dinner chaos can be largely eradicated if kids are helping make dinner. Kids love feeling grown up and are more content if they can see their future meal. They are also much more likely to happily eat whatever comes out of the oven if they have been part of the process.

Be aware of advertising and don't fall for it. We all know the real estate gimmicks where *cozy* means "teeny tiny" and *great for antique lovers* means "really ancient." Food advertisers have their own technically correct but highly misleading jargon and images. Play the skeptic and teach your children that advertised products are not usually as great as they seem.

Forgive yourself for slip-ups. Just get back up and keep going. Stay honest about writing down what you spend. Keeping track of extra expenditures reinforces the fact that you can do it if you give up those things. Write down the extra pizza or dinner out and you will know what you could have saved if you had chosen to do without. Let that be an incentive for the next month.

You really can be successful at feeding your family for less, saving for something you want, learning new skills, and becoming more self-reliant.

18. Summary of Tips

The labor and sweat of our brows is so far from being a curse that without it our very bread would not be so great a blessing. . . . If it were not for labor, men could neither eat so much, nor relish so pleasantly, nor sleep so soundly, nor be so healthful, so useful, so strong, so patient, so noble, nor so untempted.

—Jeremy Taylor

Here is a quick check-list of things we have covered in more detail in the book. At different readings you will be ready to try different ideas, so you should refer back to this list often. Check off the things you are working on and are already doing. Be inspired and save money!

- ☐ Go to the store less often. Try to make do with what you have.
- ☐ Make a menu for the month.
- ☐ Create a master grocery list with everything you need for the whole month. Take it shopping with you.
- ☐ Estimate your costs and leave some money for unexpected expenses.
- ☐ Set a grocery budget and keep track of how much you have spent. Stay within your budget.
- ☐ Keep a running list of things you need at the store so you can add it to your master list next month.
- ☐ Use beans, rice, potatoes, and whole grains as the base of your meals.
- ☐ Make things from scratch instead of mixes or boxes.
- ☐ Before you buy, decide if you can make it yourself.
- ☐ Make your own bread.

- ☐ Buy the least expensive fruits and vegetables.
- ☐ Check clearance shelves at your store.
- ☐ Buy things on sale and change the menu accordingly.
- ☐ Anticipate sale items when planning your menu.
- ☐ Compare price per unit before buying bulk or things "on sale."
- ☐ Preserve free food for future use.
- ☐ Get a freezer—for cheap.
- ☐ Double your recipe and freeze the second dish for future use.
- ☐ Quit spending money on snacks.
- ☐ Buy bulk and divide into portions.
- ☐ Add extra water to juice and milk.
- ☐ Grease muffin tins instead of using liners.
- ☐ Wash dishes by hand instead of using the dishwasher.
- ☐ Use dryer sheets more than once.
- ☐ Buy store brands instead of name brands.
- ☐ Present food so a little looks like a lot.
- ☐ Drink water with your meals.
- ☐ Use half the meat called for in a recipe.
- ☐ Use bouillon instead of meat.
- ☐ Cut down on expensive dairy intake.
- ☐ Keep breakfast and lunch simple and inexpensive.
- ☐ Eat hot cereals instead of cold, boxed cereals.
- ☐ Create your own recipes from ingredients you have.
- ☐ Be generous and do unto others as you would have done unto you.

Recipes and Ideas

This section has lists of menu ideas and a few basic filler recipes to get you started. The recipes include some of my favorites that are not too common, or my twist on a common recipe. There are hundreds of recipe books and online resources for more ideas. Besides traditional family recipes, I use three cookbooks that are in line with the way I feed my family. They are informative, use basic ingredients, and produce delicious results. I highly recommend all of them.

- ¿ *366 Delicious Ways to Cook Rice, Beans, and Grains* by Andrea Chesman discusses almost every bean and grain variety there is. Every recipe I have tried has been successful and delicious.

- ¿ *Whole Foods for the Whole Family* published by La Leche League International has great family recipes from different countries. It covers original basics like sprouts and yogurt making. Kids can get involved in many of the recipes.

- ¿ *Better Homes and Gardens* (the red and white book that has been a part of almost every home since the 1950s). It's a good all-around book for cooking. My older version covers nutrition, meal planning, cuts of meat and how to cook them, canning and preserving, barbecuing, plus recipes for the basics—sauces, soups, cakes, breads, and so forth.

Remember that many recipes can be altered to fit your needs and ingredients. My husband likes to joke that I rarely make the same thing twice. Finding a good recipe and tweaking it to fit inexpensive things I have is easy and (usually) rewarding. Please not that unless otherwise noted, these recipes make 6–8 servings.

Breakfasts

We keep breakfast simple and quick for the weekdays without resorting to expensive and milk-consuming cold cereals. On the weekends we have more time to make pancakes, waffles, coffee cakes—whatever we feel like. Muffins and quick breads like banana bread, can be made in the evening or on a baking day and frozen. They thaw overnight or quickly in the microwave for a weekday breakfast. Here are some of our weekday staples with a few recipes.

Breakfast Ideas

Oatmeal
Rice with Raisins
Grits
Toast with fruit or applesauce
Soft-boiled eggs on toast
Hard-boiled eggs in hard rolls
Banana bread/muffins with fruit
Scrambled eggs and toast

Breakfast Recipes

Good Ol' Oatmeal

4 cups water
2 cups regular rolled oats
¼ cup brown sugar

Bring water to boil. Pour in oats and turn off stove, but leave pan on burner. Let sit for five minutes. Stir in brown sugar and serve with milk. Serves 6–8.

Rice with Raisins

4 cups water
2 cups white rice
⅔ cup raisins

⅓ cup white sugar

Bring water and rice to boil and reduce heat. Simmer, covered, for 20 minutes, or until rice is cooked. Stir in raisins and sugar. Serve with milk. Serves 8.

Egg Tips and Tricks

Soft-boiled: Place eggs in cold water on the stove. Bring water to boiling. When water starts boiling, continue to boil for three minutes (set a timer!). Remove eggs from heat and run cold water in the pan to stop cooking. To serve, break eggs in half with a knife and scoop out insides with a spoon onto toast.

Hard-boiled: Place eggs in cold water on the stove. Bring to boiling. Boil ten minutes. Serve hot. We like to eat hard-boiled eggs in a hollowed out roll. Slice the roll in half like a hamburger bun and eat out the inside. Butter the hollowed-out roll, add peeled hot egg, salt, put roll halves together and eat like a sandwich.

Scrambled: Break six eggs in mixing bowl. Add ⅓ cup milk. Beat with a fork until egg whites and yolks break up and mix together. Melt 1 tablespoon butter in skillet. Add eggs and cook on medium heat stirring occasionally with spatula. Add salt and pepper to taste. Remove from heat when eggs are cooked but still slightly moist.

Lunches
· · · · · · · · · · · · ·

Lunch at our house is usually peanut butter and jelly sandwiches with fruit and/or carrot sticks. We eat leftovers only if there isn't enough for another dinner. There is no need to make a complete meal at lunchtime. PBJs and fruit require little expense and no planning. Save your cooking energy for a good dinner!

Dinners

· · · · · · · · · · · · ·

This section is divided into the four fillers. Remember to make sure you have the necessary food groups represented at dinner. Enhance these basic ideas with fruit, bread, and veggies if they aren't included in the main dish.

Rice Ideas

Stir-fry
Spanish Rice
Sweet and Sour
Curry
Pilaf
Missionary Rice
Chicken Soup with Rice
Fried Rice

Rice Recipes
• • • • • • • • • • • • • • •

Cooking Rice ··

Rice requires a 1:2 ratio with water. For example, one cup of rice needs to cook in two cups of water. You can feed one person with ⅓ cup of uncooked rice. Combine rice and water in a covered pot. Cook over high heat until boiling and then reduce heat to low. Simmer 20 minutes for white rice and 45 minutes for brown rice.

Rice Pilaf ·······································

Pilafs are extremely versatile. Just look at how many boxed options are in the stores! Here is a basic recipe for six people.

2 cups rice	1 clove crushed garlic
4 cups water	1 Tbsp. dried parsley
4 cubes chicken boullion	

In saucepan, combine all ingredients. Heat to a slow boil, reduce heat to low. Cook according to directions in "Cooking Rice" above. Fluff with fork and serve.

You may add a can of mushrooms, chopped broccoli, mixed veggies, or other things you have that sound good. Beef bullion may also be substituted for chicken bullion.

Missionary Rice ································

Missionary rice is a simple recipe I made up while serving a mission for my church. My husband and kids enjoy both the dish and its name.

½ lb. hamburger or sausage	1½ cups rice
1 onion chopped	3 cups water
1 Tbsp. dried dill	

Brown meat and onion in skillet. Add rice, water, and dill. Cook according to directions in "Cooking Rice" above. Season with salt and pepper before serving. Pass plain yogurt at the table for diners to put on top of rice.

Stir-Fry Rice ....

A versatile and simple meal, stir-fry can be made with almost any vegetables you have on hand. I've done stir-fry with countless combinations of celery, onions, broccoli, cauliflower, carrots, cabbage, snow peas, corn, and peppers. Meat is optional. If you choose to use meat—chicken, beef, hamburger, or sausage—brown it first in a little oil in a large pot. Add the veggies and put the lid on. If you use only veggies, put a little oil in the bottom of the pot. They should steam for about 12–15 minutes. Season with soy sauce, salt, and pepper. If you want a nice sauce, add a little beef bullion and 2 tablespoons cornstarch mixed with 2 tablespoons cold water to the cooked vegetables. Serve over plain cooked rice and pass around the soy sauce at the table.

Spanish Rice ....

1 onion, chopped	1½ cups rice
1 clove garlic, crushed	3 cups water
3 cubes chicken bouillon	1 can diced tomatoes
	1 tsp. cumin
3 Tbsp. butter or margarine	1 Tbsp. dried parsley
	salt and pepper

Sauté onion, garlic and chicken bouillon in butter or margarine. Add rice. Stir and sauté until rice and onion are translucent, about 5 minutes. Add water, tomatoes, cumin, and parsley. Cook according to "Cooking Rice" directions on page 54 until rice is done and water is absorbed. Season with salt and pepper to taste.

Sweet and Sour ·······································

This Sweet and Sour sauce works with any kind of meat, and even without meat if you choose. Cut meat into chunks and season with salt and pepper. Dredge in flour and brown in pan with a little oil. If you have ground meat, you can make simple meatballs and brown them. Make the sauce right on top of the browned meat in the pan.

1 (20–oz.) can pineapple tidbits, undrained	¾ cup brown sugar
¾ cup ketchup	2 Tbsp. white sugar
	¼ cup vinegar

Combine pineapple tidbits, ketchup, brown sugar, white sugar, and vinegar in a medium saucepan. If desired, add chopped onion, green pepper, and carrots, and simmer till vegetables are crisp-tender. Add 2 tablespoons cornstarch mixed with 2 tablespoons cold water to thicken before serving. Serve over rice.

Chicken Curry ·······································

½ onion, chopped	1 cup diced cooked chicken (optional)
2 Tbsp. butter or margarine	2 Tbsp. curry powder
3 Tbsp. flour	1 cup diced potatoes
4 cups water	1 cup diced carrots
4 cubes chicken bouillon	2 Tbsp. lemon juice
	2 egg yolks, beaten

In saucepan, sauté onion in butter or margarine. Add flour. Slowly stir in water and simmer until thickened. Transfer to crock pot and add chicken (optional), chicken bouillon, curry powder, potatoes, and carrots. Cook on low 6–8 hours. Before serving, add some sauce to beaten egg yolks in a small bowl, then whisk egg-sauce mix into remainder of sauce. Add 2 tablespoons lemon juice. Serve over rice.

Lemony Chicken Rice Soup ································

Our kids love chicken rice soup. It's always a big hit at our house thanks to the poem by Maurice Sendak, "Chicken Soup With Rice." Then, at a restaurant one time, my husband and I tasted a chicken rice soup with a little lemon. It was so delicious, we attempted to make something similar at home. This is the yummy result.

½ large onion, chopped
1 clove garlic, crushed
1½ cup rice
2 Tbsp. butter or margarine
12 cups water
1½ cups cooked cubed chicken
10 cubes chicken bouillon
1 Tbsp. dried parsley
½ tsp. dried dill
1½ Tbsp. lemon juice

In a 6-quart stock pot, sauté onion, garlic, and rice in butter or margarine until rice and onion are translucent. Add water, cubed chicken, bouillon (or equivalent), parsley, and dill. Simmer until rice is tender. Add lemon juice. Salt and pepper to taste. I often use the water in which I cook the chicken for this recipe. Broth may be substituted for water and bouillon.

Fried Rice ···

Fried rice is a great catch-all dish. Almost any leftover meat can be substituted for the ham, and any vegetables compliment the rice and soy sauce. I have even made this dish without meat and the results are always good.

1 clove garlic, chopped
1 onion, chopped
3 Tbsp. oil
4 cups rice, cooked
1 cup ham, chopped
1½ cups mixed veggies, lightly steamed
soy sauce
2 eggs
salt and pepper to taste

Sauté garlic and onion in oil over medium heat until translucent. Add rice, meat, and vegetables. Cook over medium-high heat, stirring frequently with spatula. Sprinkle soy sauce over rice while cooking. Add eggs and mix quickly into rice. Keep stirring until eggs are cooked. Salt and pepper to taste.

Beans Ideas

Baked Beans
Tacos with Refried Beans
Chili
Tamale Pie
Lentil Soup
Split Pea Soup
Bean Soup
Pitas with Hummus
Taco Salad
Red Beans and Rice
Bean Salad

Bean Recipes

Soaking Beans

Before cooking, beans should be soaked. If you think ahead, you can put dry beans in a pot, cover them with twice as much water as beans, and let them sit on the counter overnight. There is also a quick-soak method you can use the day of cooking. Put the beans and water in a pot on the stove and bring to a boil. Turn the stove off and let the beans sit on the burner for an hour. For both methods you should drain the soaking water and cook in clean water.

Which Beans?

There are many dried bean varieties. Different types work best in certain dishes. We are used to seeing red kidney beans in chili and navy beans in baked beans. However, most varieties can be used in most dishes. While all dried beans are fairly inexpensive, kidney and pinto are easy to find in bulk and are, therefore, usually the most cost effective. They will work for most bean recipes you find.

Baked Beans

2 cups dried pinto
  beans, soaked
8 cups water
1 large onion, chopped
½ cup maple syrup
½ cup ketchup

1 Tbsp. prepared
  mustard
1 tsp. ground ginger
½ cup brown sugar
¼ cup BBQ sauce
salt and pepper

Drain beans and combine with water. Simmer on low about 2 hours until tender. Add onion and simmer ½ hour until onion is tender. Drain excess liquid and add remaining ingredients. Let flavors blend for ½ hour before serving. This is a good crock-pot recipe. Cook beans 6–8 hours and add other ingredients the last hour or so.

Refried Beans..

2 cups dried pinto
  beans, soaked
8 cups water
2 Tbsp. oil
2 tsp. minced garlic

1 onion, chopped
½ tsp. chili powder
1½ tsp. cumin
salt and pepper

Drain beans and cook in water until tender, about 2 hours. Drain and reserve extra liquid. Sauté onion, garlic, and seasonings in oil. Add to beans. Mash with potato masher, adding reserved liquid as necessary to get proper consistency. Add salt and pepper to taste. **In the crock-pot:** Cook beans in the crock-pot for 6–8 hours and add remaining ingredients in the last hour before mashing.

Chili ....

4 cups dried kidney
  beans, soaked
10 cups water
2 onions, chopped
1 Tbsp. minced garlic
1 green bell pepper,
  diced

1 Tbsp. chili powder
1 Tbsp. cumin
2 Tbsp. oil
3 cups diced tomatoes
¼ cup corn meal
salt and pepper

Cook beans in water until tender, about 2 hours. Sauté onion, garlic, bell pepper, chili powder, and cumin in oil. Add to beans. Add tomatoes and whisk in corn meal. Cook for 30 minutes. Adjust seasonings to taste.

Lentil Soup ....

Lentils are little known beans that are cheap and easy to cook. This yummy recipe is one of our favorite soups.

2 cups lentils
8 cups water
½ cup onion, chopped
½ cup celery, chopped
¼ cup carrots, chopped
1 Tbsp. dried parsley

1 clove garlic, minced
2½ tsp. salt
¼ tsp. pepper
½ tsp. oregano
1 can diced tomatoes
2 Tbsp. vinegar

Rinse lentils; drain and place in soup kettle. Add remaining ingredients except tomatoes and vinegar. Cover and simmer 1½ hours. Add tomatoes and vinegar. Simmer, covered, 30 minutes longer.

Tamale Pie ....

Tamale pie is basically chili with corn bread baked on top. If you don't have leftover chili, mix cooked beans with canned tomatoes, dried onions and a little chili powder. Serve with your favorite corn bread recipe. You can add cheese on top of the corn bread before baking if you like, or serve it on the side. Bake as per corn bread directions. Serve with fresh lettuce and sour cream.

Split Pea Soup ....

1 lb. split peas
1 bay leaf
1 chopped onion
1 clove minced garlic
4 medium chopped carrots
¼ tsp. thyme

2 stalks celery
10 cups water
4 cubes chicken bouillon OR ham bone OR chopped ham

Put all ingredients in a crock pot in the morning and cook 8 hours. Pull the ham bone (if used) and bay leaf. Process remainder in food processor. Return to crock pot with cut up meat (if used). Salt and pepper to taste.

Bean Soup ....

2 cups dried beans
1 chopped onion
2 chopped carrots
2 stalks chopped celery
2 cloves minced garlic

1 cup chopped ham or ham bone, or 4 cubes chicken bouillon
salt and pepper

Soak beans overnight. Rinse. Cover with 8 cups water and simmer until soft—usually 2–3 hours. Add rest of ingredients and simmer another hour. Salt and pepper to taste.

Hummus ....

This bean dip is delicious on both breads and raw vegetables. It can be eaten warm or cold.

3 cups cooked
  garbanzo beans
3 Tbsp. peanut butter
2 tsp. chicken bouillon
3 Tbsp. sesame seeds
2 Tbsp. parsley flakes

3 cloves garlic
2 Tbsp. lemon juice
1 Tbsp. soy sauce
extra bean juice
salt and pepper

Process all ingredients in a blender. Add bean juice to make a smooth paste. Salt and pepper to taste.

Pasta Ideas

Spaghetti
Tuna Noodle Casserole
Lasagna
Pasta Salad
Chicken Noodle Soup
Stroganoff
Cowboy Casserole
Vegetable Beef Soup with Noodles

Pasta Recipes

Tuna Noodle Casserole

This dish is an easy kids' favorite in our home. Cook 1 pound noodles of your choice. Drain and return to pot. Add 1 can of tuna (with liquid) and 1 can creamed chicken or creamed mushroom soup. Stir, then add salt and pepper to taste. Sprinkle cheese on top and cover. Let sit on low heat for 5–10 minutes until cheese is melted. Serve.

Lasagna

1 lb. ground meat or sausage
1 chopped onion
2 cups cottage cheese
2 eggs
1 Tbsp. Italian seasoning

⅓ cup Parmesan cheese
4 cups spaghetti sauce
1 cup shredded cheese
1 lb. box lasagna noodles

Brown meat with onion until meat and onion are cooked. Add 2 cups sauce to meat mixture. In a medium bowl, mix cottage cheese, eggs, Italian seasoning, and Parmesan cheese. Spoon a small amount spaghetti sauce to cover the bottom of 9x13 pan. Noodles may be cooked or dry. Layer the following: noodles, ½ of the meat mixture, noodles, ½ cheese mixture, noodles, rest of meat mixture, noodles, rest of cheese mixture, noodles, and remaining sauce. Cover tightly and bake for 1 hour at 350 degrees. Sprinkle shredded cheese on top and bake, uncovered, until cheese melts and browns (about 10–15 minutes).

Chicken Noodle Soup ....

A great soup for cold days or when you feel a sore throat coming on. Sauté some chicken chunks and garlic in a little oil. Add chicken broth or water and 1 teaspoon bouillon for each cup water. Add chopped onion, carrots, celery, and parsley. Simmer until vegetables are cooked. Add noodles 15 minutes before serving. This is a great soup for homemade noodles. Salt and pepper to taste. For extra thickness whisk in a little corn-starch mixed with an equal amount of cold water.

To make a vegetable beef soup, use beef broth or bouillon instead of chicken. Add leftover roast or shredded beef instead of chicken chunks. Potatoes or rice can be substituted for the noodles. Add them with the rest of the vegetables at the beginning.

Stroganoff ....

½ lb. ground beef
1 chopped onion
1 clove minced garlic
3 Tbsp. flour
1 can creamed
  mushroom soup

1 can mushrooms
½ cup sour cream
salt and pepper

Sauté meat with onion and garlic. Add flour and mix into meat. Add 3 cups water and cook, stirring, until gravy thickens. Add soup and mushrooms with juice, and cook, stirring, until gravy thickens. Add sour cream and heat through. Add salt and pepper to taste. Serve over noodles.

Cowboy Casserole ....

1 lb. elbow macaroni
½ lb. ground meat
1 chopped onion

1 can corn
1 can tomatoes
2 cups spaghetti sauce

Cook noodles. Drain. In pot, brown meat with onion. Add noodles, corn, tomatoes, and spaghetti sauce. Salt and pepper to taste.

Potatoes Ideas
• • • • • • • • • • • • •

Hamburger Gravy over Potatoes
Baked Potatoes
Potato Wedges
Clam Chowder
Hamburger Pie
Pot Pie
Vegetable Beef Soup with Potatoes
Stew
Autumn Soup
Mashed Potatoes with or without Gravy
Potato Salad

Potato Recipes

Cooking Potatoes

Baked Potatoes: Scrub potatoes in cold water, prick with a fork, and bake at 350 degrees for 1½ hours. If you want a softer skin that is easier to eat, wrap them in foil before baking. Hint: It takes less foil if you wrap them diagonally instead of straight.

Mashed Potatoes: Peel (if desired) and dice 5 or 6 medium potatoes. Cover potatoes with water in a large pan. Simmer covered for 15 minutes, or until soft. Drain water, add ½ to 1 stick of margarine, ¼ cup milk, and salt and pepper to taste. Mash with potato masher or mix in mixer. Sour cream and chives may also be added for extra flavor. These mashed potatoes can be eaten without gravy and are delicious.

Boiled potatoes: *These are easier than mashed potatoes and are very good with gravy (see simple recipe in this section).* Scrub potatoes and cut into large cubes (a whole potato into 4–6 pieces). Cover with water and simmer, covered, until potatoes are fork tender. Drain water and serve with gravy.

Potato Wedges: Scrub and cut 5–6 potatoes into wedges. Put in large bowl. Sprinkle with 4 tablespoons oil. Add ½ teaspoon garlic powder, ¼ teaspoon pepper, 1 teaspoon onion salt, 1 tablespoon parsley flakes, and ½ cup flour. Put lid on bowl and shake until coated. Spread on a greased baking sheet and bake at 400 degrees for 20–30 minutes until fork tender and browned. Turn every 8–10 minutes while baking so they will brown evenly. Salt to taste and serve with ketchup.

Hamburger Gravy..

½ lb. hamburger	4 cubes beef bouillon
1 chopped onion	2 Tbsp. cornstarch
4 cups water	salt and pepper

Brown hamburger with onion in saucepan. Add water and bouillon. Mix cornstarch with 1½ tablespoons cold water in a cup. Whisk slowly into simmering gravy. Season with salt and pepper. Serve over potatoes.

Note: This recipe also makes a great beef broccoli. Add chopped fresh or frozen broccoli to gravy before adding cornstarch, and let it simmer until the broccoli is tender–crisp. Add cornstarch mixture to thicken and serve over rice.

Basic Chowder ....

A chowder is a basic potato soup. Different ingredients are added to the potatoes to create a variety of yummy soups.

5 medium potatoes	2 stalks chopped celery
1 chopped onion	4 Tbsp. butter
1 clove minced garlic	¼ cup flour
4 tsp. chicken bouillon	3 cups milk

Peel and dice potatoes. Put in pot and simmer, covered, until fork tender. Meanwhile, in saucepan, sauté onions, garlic, celery, and bouillon in butter until translucent. Add flour and stir to make a paste. Slowly stir in milk and cook until thickened. Add flour mixture to simmering potatoes. Stir until mixed and thickened. Salt and pepper to taste.

Clam chowder: Sauté clams (and juice) with onion mixture. After combining with potatoes, add 1½ tablespoons dill weed. May cook diced carrots with the potatoes as well.

Country potato soup: Omit butter. Brown ½ lb. sausage or 4 strips bacon. Sauté onions, garlic, celery, and bouillon in meat fat. If using bacon, crumble before adding to soup. After combining with potatoes, mix in 2 tablespoons parsley and 1 cup shredded cheddar cheese.

Corn chowder: Add one can creamed corn and heat before serving.

Hamburger Pie ....

½ lb. ground meat
1 chopped onion
2–3 cups spaghetti
  sauce
2 cans green beans

leftover mashed
  potatoes
¾ cup shredded
  cheddar cheese

Brown meat and onion. Add spaghetti sauce and beans. Spread out in 9x13 pan. Spoon leftover mashed potatoes on top, covering meat. Sprinkle with cheese. Bake at 350 degrees for 30 minutes.

Pot Pies ....

Pot pies are a great winter meal. One pie can fill a whole family for dinner. There are as many varieties as there are cooks, so I will only give a basic idea here. Get online or look in any cookbook if you want a specific recipe. The main idea is to cook any meat and vegetables you want in it, and mix them with a cream soup or a flour/butter/bouillon roux (like you make soups with) and put it all in a pie crust. Leftover soups, if they are thick enough, also work well as pie filling. Most pies bake for an hour at 350 degrees. Look in the dessert section for an easy no-fail pie-crust recipe. Another version of pot pie is to put the filling in a square or oblong baking pan and cover the top with biscuit dough. Either way, the result is a yummy family dinner.

Stew ....

½ lb. burger or stew
  meat
1 chopped onion
3 sliced carrots
3 diced potatoes

1 clove minced garlic
4 tsp. beef bouillon
2 Tbsp. flour
1½ cups water
salt and pepper

Brown meat. Put in crock pot with everything but flour. Cook until vegetables are tender, about 6 hours on low. Sprinkle flour on top and mix in. Cook until thickened. Salt and pepper to taste.

Autumn Soup ....

½ lb. ground beef
1 onion, chopped
2 stalks celery,
  chopped
2 carrots, diced
3 potatoes, diced
8 cups water

½ tsp. pepper
3 tsp. salt
1 tsp. basil
2 bay leaves
2 tsp. beef bouillon
1 can diced tomatoes

Brown ground beef and onion in large pot. Add everything but tomatoes. Simmer, covered, 20 minutes. Add tomatoes. Simmer 10 more minutes. Adjust seasonings.

Potato Salad ....

4–5 potatoes
3 eggs
3 stalks chopped celery
½ medium onion, minced
¼ cup minced dill
  pickles

2 tsp. salt
1 cup mayonnaise
2 Tbsp. mustard
1 tsp. sugar
¼ cup plus 2 Tbsp.
  milk

Boil whole potatoes and eggs until fork goes into potatoes easily, about 20 minutes. Drain and let cool. Peel and dice cooled potatoes and eggs in large bowl. Add celery, onion, and pickles. Sprinkle with salt. Mix together. In separate bowl, combine mayonnaise, mustard, sugar, and milk. Stir into potatoes. Add more salt if necessary.

Whole Grains

A note about white and wheat flour: any recipe that calls for flour will work with part whole-wheat flour. Using all whole-wheat will usually work as well; however, the end result may be a little heavier and have more nutty wheat flavor than you want. Most families will enjoy the change from white to wheat if a little is added in all foods containing flour rather than using all white in some recipes and all wheat in others. Try adding half wheat flour to biscuits, pancakes, rolls, crusts, even cookies and cakes.

Ideas

Waffles
German Pancakes
Hamburgers
Hot Dogs
Navajo Tacos
Crepes
Pizza
Fried Corn Meal Mush w/ Syrup
Spoon Bread
Corn Bread
Scones
Biscuits and Gravy
Pot Pie
Creamed Eggs on Toast

Whole Grain Recipes
• •

Multigrain Waffles..

This delicious recipe from my mother-in-law is hearty enough for a good dinner. I serve them with pureed frozen fruit as a topping and a vegetable-filled omelet on the side.

1½ cups whole-wheat flour
1 cup old fashioned rolled oats
¾ cup cornmeal
4 tsp. baking powder
¾ tsp. salt
1½ Tbsp. sugar
2 eggs
½ cup cooking oil
2 cups water

Mix all dry ingredients. Add wet ingredients and mix. Wait 10 minutes for oatmeal to thicken before cooking.

Whole Wheat Bread...

½ cup hot tap water
3 Tbsp. yeast
5 cups hot tap water
5 cups whole-wheat flour
2 Tbsp. salt
⅔ cup oil
⅔ cup sugar or honey
5–8 cups white flour

In small bowl soften yeast in ½ cup hot tap water. In mixing bowl, put 5 cups hot water, salt, and whole-wheat flour. Mix. Add sugar and oil. Mix. Add softened yeast mixture. Mix. Add remaining flour a little at a time and knead in. Stop when you have a good bread dough consistency—moist but no longer too sticky to hold some shape. Knead for 10 minutes. Shape into 5 loaves and put in greased bread pans. Let rise until double, about 30–40 minutes. Bake at 350 degrees for 35 minutes. Turn out onto towel and butter tops to keep them soft.

Quick Hamburger Buns...

This recipe is a family favorite. We make all our own hamburger and hot dog buns. They turn out light and delicious. It is also pretty good for dinner rolls. It is so fast, I can make these rolls for dinner in the time it takes to prepare the rest of the meal. For variety, I have added herbs and cottage cheese, pumpkin and pumpkin spice, and raisins and cinnamon, all with good results. This recipe works well with part whole-wheat flour. This is also a great recipe for Navajo tacos and scones.

2 Tbsp. yeast	¼ cup sugar
1 cup + 2 Tbsp. warm water	1 egg
	1 tsp. salt
⅓ cup oil	3–3½ cup flour

Dissolve yeast in water. Add oil and sugar. Let stand 5 minutes. Add egg, salt, and flour to make soft dough. Knead 3–5 minutes. Do not let rise. Shape into 12 balls. Place 3 inches apart on greased cookie sheet. Cover and let rest for 10 minutes (while oven is heating). Bake at 425 degrees for 8–12 minutes. Cool on wire rack.

For Scones or Navajo Tacos: Roll out the dough on a floured surface and cut into 3-inch squares for scones or 5 inch circles for Navajo tacos. Fry in hot oil and drain on plate covered with paper towels. Serve with butter and honey or jam for scones. Serve with chili, lettuce, grated cheese, and Ranch dressing for Navajo tacos. Yum!

French Bread/Pizza Dough ....

½ cup hot tap water
2 Tbsp. yeast
4 cups hot tap water

2 Tbsp. salt
7–8 cups flour (may mix
wheat and white)

In small bowl soften yeast in ½ cup hot tap water.

In mixing bowl mix 4 cups hot tap water with salt and 4 cups flour. Mix in softened yeast mixture. Add flour a little at a time and knead in. Stop when you have a good bread dough consistency. Knead 5–6 minutes.

For French bread: Shape into long loaves and put on greased cookie sheets. With knife, make diagonal slashes across top. Raise for 30 minutes. Bake at 350 degrees for 30 minutes. Butter tops.

For pizza dough: Grease two jelly roll pans. Sprinkle cornmeal over grease. Divide dough in half and spread out on pans to form crust. Let rest 10 minutes. Bake for 8 minutes in 400-degree oven. Put toppings on, and continue baking for 12–15 minutes until cheese is bubbly and browning.

Desserts

Desserts make memories. Hot homemade doughnuts on a cozy fall afternoon or homemade pies for the holidays are things we don't forget. Desserts shouldn't be a part of every meal, but a sweet treat once in a while adds spice to life.

Ideas

Cakes
Cookies
Homemade Popsicles
Graham Crackers with Frosting
Fruit—Canned or Fresh
Pies
Homemade Doughnuts
Pie Dough Cookies

Recipes
········

No-Fail Pie Crust ....

2/3 cups shortening
2 cups flour
1 tsp. salt
7 Tbsp. cold water

Cut shortening into flour and salt. Add water while mixing. Mix just until water is incorporated. Do not over-mix. Divide in half. Roll out each half between two sheets of waxed paper or plastic wrap. Makes a two crust pie.

Pie-Dough Cookies: Place leftover pie crust cuttings on an ungreased cookie sheet. Sprinkle with cinnamon and sugar. Bake at 350 degrees for 8–10 minutes.

Homemade Doughnuts ....

2 cups milk
4 Tbsp. oil
5 Tbsp. sugar
2½ Tbsp. yeast

½ Tbsp. salt
½ tsp. nutmeg
4–5 cups flour

Scald milk in saucepan, and transfer it to a mixing bowl. Add oil and sugar. Add yeast when milk has slightly cooled (to hot tap water temperature). Let sit 5 minutes to soften yeast. Add salt, nutmeg, and most of flour. Add remaining flour slowly while kneading until dough is rolling consistency. Roll out on floured surface. Cut doughnuts. Let rise 10 minutes. Fry in hot oil. Dip in cinnamon sugar or glaze.

Sources
·········

1. ScienceDaily, "Price and Taste Trump Nutrition when Americans Eat Out," October 23, 2007, http://www.sciencedaily.com/releases/2007/10/071022120256.htm

2. ScienceDaily, "'Convenience' Foods Save Little Time for Working Families at Dinner," August 13, 2007, http://www.sciencedaily.com/releases/2007/08/070807135415.htm

3. United States Department of Agriculture, "MyPyramid.gov: Steps to a Healthier You," http://www.mypyramid.gov.

4. Natural Resources Defence Council, "Exploding Sales—Marketing a Perception of Purity," in *Bottled Water: Pure Drink or Pure Hype?* http://www.nrdc.org/water/drinking/bw/chap2.asp

5. Gregory Karp, "Tap Water Might Fit Your Bill Better than Bottled Water," Sun Sentinal. http://www.sun-sentinel.com/business/sns-yourmoney-0910spending,0,3316261.story?coll=sns-ap-basketball-headlines&track=mostemailedlink

6. Asian Food Information Centre, "The Secrets to a Longer Life," in Food Facts Asia, Issue 32, March 31, 2008, http://www.afic.org/FFA%20Issue%2032%20The%20Secret%20to%20a%20Longer%20Life_Eng.htm

7. Hilaire Belloc, "The Vulture," *The Book of Virtues: A Treasury of Great Moral Stories*. Edited by William J Bennett (New York: Simon & Schuster, 1993) 46.

Blank Menus

Sunday	Monday	Tuesday	Wednesday	Thursday	Friday

Sunday	Monday	Tuesday	Wednesday	Thursday	Friday

Blank Menus

Sunday	Monday	Tuesday	Wednesday	Thursday	Friday

Sunday	Monday	Tuesday	Wednesday	Thursday	Friday

Notes

Notes

Notes

Notes

About the Author

L orae Bowden is the oldest of eleven children. While growing up, she learned homemaking skills from her mother. As a senior in high school, she was the Homemaking Sterling Scholar. She graduated from Brigham Young University with a BS in elementary education and enjoyed teaching preschool, first grade, and fifth grade. Since the birth of her first baby, she has stayed home to be a mother. She and her husband, Jared, are the parents of seven children. They live in Bozeman, Montana.